EMILIE TAVERNIER GAMELIN

André-M. Cimichella, o.s.m.
Auxiliary Bishop Emeritus of Montreal

EMILIE TAVERNIER GAMELIN

The Great Lady of Montreal
Foundress of the Sisters of Providence

CARTE **BLANCHE**

Les Éditions Carte blanche
1209, avenue Bernard Ouest
Bureau 200
Outremont (Québec)
H2V 1V7
Tel. : (514) 276-1298
fax : (514) 276-1349
E-mail : carteblanche@vl.videotron.ca

Distribution in Canada
FIDES
165, rue Deslauriers
Saint-Laurent (Québec)
H4N 2S4
Tel. : (514) 745-4290
Fax : (514) 745-4299

Legal deposit : february 2002
Bibliothèque nationale du Québec
ISBN 2-922291-83-9

Sculpture of Mr Raoul Hunter placed
in the Metro Station of Berri-UQAM
May 2000

"Sustained by the merits of my Savior,
I am filled with hope."

MOTHER GAMELIN

Reproduction of the Pieta which adorns
the tomb of Blessed Emilie Tavernier Gamelin.

To the Reader,

On the 31st of May 1981, feast of the Visitation of Our Lady, Archbishop Paul Grégoire, Archbishop of Montreal, celebrated a solemn Mass of thanksgiving in Notre Dame Church during which he promulgated the official decree opening the Cause of Beatification of Mother Gamelin.

It was the first time, following the new post-conciliar dispositions of Pope Paul VI in his motu proprio "Sanctitas Clarior"[1] that such an event took place in Montreal.

Since the publication of that document, and with the permission of the Holy See, a local bishop in his own diocese may now promulgate a Beatification Cause. What joy! What hope! Mother Gamelin on the way to official glorification!

* * *

Since 1927, when I was only six years old, every day of the week, morning and evening, for five years, I passed in front of "l'Asile de la Providence" at the corner of Saint Catherine and Saint Hubert Streets. I was going to Our Lady of Mount Carmel Elementary School, accompanied at first by my older sister and then later on, I would accompany my younger sister. I used to notice even then the imposing and venerable edifice of the Sisters of Providence and I realize that Mother

---

1. March 19, 1969.

Gamelin, who had lived and died there, and who rested in the chapel, already had her eyes fixed upon me.

Nearly twenty years later, in the summer of 1946, I was appointed as curate in this very parish of my childhood and I began to associate regularly with the Sisters of Providence. For four years I also had the opportunity to preach the regular monthly retreat at the Bourget Hospice in the Hochelaga district. When I was later transferred to Winnipeg, I was more than adequately equipped with sermons, which I regularly used for several religious communities during my five years in the Canadian West.

On my return to Montreal in 1955, as pastor of the parish of Our Lady of Mount Carmel, it was a joy to find the Sisters of Providence once again. We often celebrated the feast of Our Lady of Sorrows together. I made so many visits to the residents, to the workshop and to the chapel! What memories! What profitable meetings!

Two young students at Saint Mary's College, former boarders with the Sisters of Providence, discovered their religious vocations in the Order of Servites of Mary. One of these priests, Father Armand Gaudreau, was rector of the Sanctuary of Our Lady of Sorrows near Gaspé and the other, Father Jean Provost, was pastor of Saint Raymond's Parish in Montreal. Two graces from Mother Gamelin!

Since the demolition of the venerable convent at the corner of Saint Catherine and Saint Hubert Streets, and especially when I was at the Cathedral in 1964, I have made many visits to the new Mother House and to the beautiful new tomb of Mother Gamelin. All this crowned by the official introduction of her Cause for Beatification. Thus, I felt an obligation to write about Mother Gamelin.

I had the good fortune to find an exceptionally good biography, dating from the very beginning of the century, written with great love by a Sister of Providence, who has remained anonymous.[2] Thus with this book open before me and my hand resting lovingly on the tomb of Mother Gamelin I have written these lines. My whole heart, beating with gratitude towards Mother Gamelin and the Sisters of Providence whom I have known through the years, is in this work.

We shall soon be able to call Mother Gamelin by the grand title of Blessed, and then one day, Saint.

Montreal
Feast of Saint Elizabeth of Hungary

---

2. *Life of Mother Gamelin,* translated by Anna T. Sadlier, Montreal, 1912.

BIRTH AND ADOLESCENCE
February 19, 1800

Near the center of the Fief of Providence, above Mount Royal Avenue, there was a modest wooden two-story house, shaded by trees and surrounded by a garden. There, on the 19th of February 1800, Emilie Tavernier was born.

Her father was Antoine Tavernier, a longtime wheelwright by trade. He enjoyed the reputation of being an upright man, pious, charitable, honest and loyal in all aspects of his life. His wife, Josephte Maurice, a woman of frail and delicate constitution, though strong and energetic in character, brought to the duties of her household and to the education of her children a zeal and ardor far beyond her strength.

God blessed the union of this truly Christian couple and fifteen children were born to them, which brought them much happiness. Of these, however, only six survived past childhood: Antoine, Josephte, Joseph, Julien, François and last of all Emilie.

To the loving and tender care of her mother, the child responded by gentle, kind ways and touching attentions. When scarcely four years old, she was already attempting to help her mother with her work. "Go and rest", she would say, "I will replace you", and seizing a long feather duster, she would pass it energetically over the various pieces of furniture in each room. Her mother encouraged this tendency and from her earliest years strove to inspire in Emilie a liking for household chores.

She also allowed Emilie to share in works of charity with her in order to develop in the heart of the child a great love for the poor.

To little Emilie was given the task of distributing the alms to the needy persons who came to the door. The family had a basket for this purpose and often, unknown to anyone, the child would put in it fruit or other delicacies that she deprived herself of in favor of the poor.

One day, she saw a poor old man coming up the steep path that led to their home. He walked very slowly leaning on his stick. Emilie seized her basket and hurried out to meet him. The old man took off his hat and taking the bag from his shoulder, held it wide open to receive the offered gift. The child eagerly emptied the entire contents of her basket into the bag; but seeing that everything she had was swallowed up by the large bag, she could not hold back her tears and ran crying to her mother, "Mama, mama, the bag isn't full!" Her mother tried to console her by explaining that the beggar's bag was purposely very large because he hoped to fill it with other gifts before evening fell so that there would be enough for his whole family. Nevertheless, Emilie's tears continued to flow. Her mother's wise reasoning had little effect on the child with such a kind and generous heart, because even though the beggar's bag was far too big she still grieved because she wanted to fill it. She would have liked to put in the bag all that she possessed.

Emilie's first great sorrow at the age of four, was the loss of her mother. She was fourteen years old when her father passed away.

Before dying, her mother confided Emilie to her sister-in-law, Mrs. Joseph Perrault, a well-to-do widow. Her cousins received her as their little sister and they strove by kind attention and affectionate care to compensate Emilie for the loss of her own home and dear ones.

A few years later, Emilie was confided to the Sisters of the Congregation of Notre Dame, whose boarding school, the only one then in existence in Montreal, was situated on Saint Jean Baptiste Street. There she continued the studies begun at home.

She always kept happy memories of her teachers, whom she liked to call "her mothers".

YOUTH AND MARRIAGE
1823

Miss Emilie Tavernier made her debut in society at the age of nineteen. Descriptions given of her at that time describe her with fine features, an erect figure with an air of distinction, glowing complexion and large, bright eyes. Her manners were attractive, marked by simplicity and freedom from constraint, enhanced by a good sense of humor, frankness and amiability, always cordial and ready to oblige. Needless to say, she was very popular and had many friends.

Emilie Tavernier was twenty-three years old when, on the 4th of June 1823, she married Jean Baptiste Gamelin in Notre Dame Church.

Mr. Gamelin was then fifty years old. On two previous occasions he had been engaged to marry. The second time, he was already at the altar but just before pronouncing the irrevocable "I do", he changed his mind. What prompted him to do this is unknown. There is no doubt, however, that if he experienced any hesitation before marrying Miss Tavernier, he never regretted his decision, for it was a union that brought perfect happiness to them both.

In her new home, Emilie found satisfaction for her ardent love of solitude and the beauties of nature. As a child, it had been her great joy to wander along the shady paths, which surrounded her father's property. At her cousin's home she had, once again, the pleasure of enjoying the freshness of the woods and the charm of the country in the large tree-filled garden at the back of the house. Her own home, surrounded by a beautiful garden, intermingled with the green undulations of other gardens and parks, and seemed to continue before finally blending into the wooded slopes of Mount Royal.

In addition, almost directly facing them was an orchard, from which Mr. Gamelin drew a considerable part of his income. Its trees produced the excellent "famous" apples, which sold for a higher price than others did and of which great quantities were exported to England.

When the weather was fine, Emilie took great delight in just walking and working in the shade of that pleasant domain.

She enjoyed these years of perfect happiness, in the quiet atmosphere of their home on Saint Antoine Street, devoting her time to her husband and children. As well she had time for the members of her own family, the friends of her childhood, and her beloved poor. These last soon learned to knock at the door of her new residence asking for donations, which her charity and her husband's wealth enabled her to bestow with even more generosity than before.

However, the death of her three children and that of her husband soon overshadowed her happiness. Her husband died, after a long illness, on the 1st of October 1827. They had been married a little more than four years. He was bitterly mourned by Emilie, his young widow, who had lavished upon him the most tender and devoted care. Jean

Baptiste had always shown the greatest kindness and tenderness to her.

Her domestic happiness was completely shattered.

Emilie was only twenty-eight years old when she found herself alone. The memory of those whom she had dearly loved and who were now parted from her, would bring tears to her eyes for the rest of her life.

These painful losses were the beginning of her vocation. Her personal sorrow would find in works of charity, solace for her grief and an outlet for her great and compassionate heart.

Her spiritual director, Father Jean Baptiste Bréguier Saint Pierre, a sulpician priest, guided her along this way. He also opened up to her a source of consolation and piety, which developed with the years. This was the devotion to Our Lady of Sorrows, which later became one of the principal devotions of her Institute.[3]

Copy of the original picture given to Emilie
by Father Bréguier St. Pierre, Sulpician, in 1828.

3. *Idem*, pages 18 to 23.

THE KIND YOUNG WIDOW
1827

Jean Baptiste Gamelin left everything to his wife and included in the bequest was a singular gift.

A few years before his marriage to Emilie, he had taken upon himself the care of a poor mentally retarded child, named Dodais. During his last illness, Jean Baptiste was worried about the future of this unfortunate lad. One day he said to his young wife, "take care of him in memory of me and of my love." She promised that she would and kept her word.

There was a time in history when persons afflicted with certain mental or physical deficiencies were seen with certain repugnance, but Emilie Gamelin accepted this legacy as a gift from God. She lodged the poor boy comfortably in a little house adjacent to her garden, and to make sure that nothing would be wanting to him, she brought his mother there, thus, at the same time, rescuing her from indigence. Emilie Gamelin often visited Dodais and bestowed upon him all the care suggested by the most delicate charity, beginning in a way a particular work, which would find such prodigious growth in the community she was to found, becoming part of the mission of the Sisters of Providence.

Heaven deigned to reward such touching devotion. Before his death, Dodais became lucid for a brief period and was able to express his gratitude towards his benefactress. In a perfectly intelligible voice, he said to her, "Madame, I thank you for all your kindness to me.

I am dying; I am going to heaven; I will pray for you." Then as if to acknowledge his mother, who was beside him, he pointed to her with his wasted hand and added, "that is my mother!" He died a few minutes later.

The charity of Mrs. Gamelin drew her especially to the aged and above all to elderly and disabled women. In her frequent visits to the homes of the poor, she had often seen these poor elderly women relegated to some corner of the house and forgotten, incapable of caring for themselves, and often spending entire days alone, frequently no one even thought to bring them food. Her sensitive heart was profoundly saddened at the sight and she often wondered how such suffering could be alleviated. Providence was not long in suggesting a solution.

Mrs. Gamelin, under the guidance of Father Saint Pierre, determined that to establish a home for the women seemed to be the will of God for her. She spoke with Father Claude Fay, a priest at the seminary and the pastor of Notre Dame Church, the only parish in existence in Montreal, at that time. She asked his assistance in procuring, in the vicinity of her own home, a place that would be suitable for the accomplishment of her charitable designs. Father Fay placed at her disposal the ground floor of a small parochial school, directed by the Sisters of the Congregation of Notre Dame, which was located at the corner of Saint Lawrence and Saint Catherine Streets. On March 4th 1830, this modest refuge was opened to the beneficiaries of the young charitable widow. To make it very evident that the work was to be for the benefit of the aged, the first person to be admitted was a woman named Madame Saint Onge, who was one hundred and two years old. Soon fifteen other elderly women, none younger than sixty, were admitted.

Mrs. Gamelin visited them every day. She attended to their needs and did a short spiritual reading with them, and often by a word or a smile, she gently but firmly settled the small conflicts that arose among them.

It was touching to see this young woman, who was endowed with all the charm that virtue lends to the gifts of nature, disregarding the mockery and criticism, while making herself the servant of the poor. She rendered them the most menial services and humbly begged alms for them in the name of Jesus.

She found strength and courage in prayer, especially in meditating on the passion of Our Lord and the sorrows of His Mother. All through her life, these were her favorite devotions. "I do not understand", she used to say, "how anyone can hesitate to make a sacrifice after having contemplated the sufferings of Jesus and the sorrows of His Blessed Mother." She made the Stations of the Cross every day with her elderly women. After the crucifix, the first object to adorn the walls of the little house on St. Philippe Street was the picture of Our Lady of Seven Dolors.

Her refuge, which soon had thirty residents, was for her meager financial resources a considerable undertaking. She had to provide for all the expenses of rent, heating, food, and clothing. Many times, when she did not know where to turn for help and was worried because her poor people would be without food, she wondered if she had not presumed too much on her own strength, and tempted Divine Providence by venturing upon a work whose future was so uncertain. But God, who feeds the birds of the air and adorns the lilies of the field, never left her without resources.

It was around this time, that Emilie Gamelin formed the excellent plan of organizing a society of ladies who would assist her in visiting the homes of the needy and in collecting the daily funds necessary for the support of the refuge. She had won the confidence of everyone. By now, her perseverance and her success silenced even those who had been very critical when she began her work. It was felt that she was fulfilling a providential mission. At the age of thirty, she had become counselor and friend to persons of every age.

The cholera epidemics of 1832 and 1834 caused terrible devastation, ravaging whole families and multiplying the number of widows and orphans. The city was plunged into consternation and mourning. The wealthy took refuge in the country or in distant cities; but the poor, forced to remain in their humble dwellings, succumbed in great numbers. A whole new area was thus opened to the charity of Emilie Gamelin who literally multiplied herself to bring assistance and comfort where needed.

Mrs. Gamelin continued her generous project in the little refuge on Saint Philippe Street for four years. Her family of poor people was increasing; the living accommodations had become much too small and the rent absorbed a considerable part of her meager resources. Filled with confidence in Divine Providence, she had recourse to prayer and had the elderly women join her in praying that some charitable person would give her a house better suited to the needs of the work.

Her faith and confidence were too great to remain unanswered. Without doubt it was God who inspired in her the idea of appealing to Mr. Olivier Berthelet, whose great charity had immortalized his name in the community of Montreal and especially in the Providence community, where he was considered one of its most distinguished benefactors.

Mrs. Gamelin invited Mr. Berthelet to visit her elderly ladies and when he arrived one of the women begged his help in such simple and moving language that his heart was touched. Without delay he made a donation to Mrs. Gamelin of a larger house situated on Saint Catherine Street near the bishop's palace.[4]

—⁂—

One day the Pastor informed the superior that he could no longer leave the Blessed Sacrament in their oratory because

4. *Idem*, pages 23 to 36.

the tabernacle door was not covered by a veil as required by the rules of the liturgy. The cash on hand amounted to fifteen shillings to cover the marketing for the week. Sister Superior, deeply distressed, conferred with her sisters and they took the unanimous decision to go without meat for eight days rather than lose the Blessed Sacrament. While the superior was in town buying the veil, a young lady came to the parlor. She told the sister who received her, "I made a promise, for a grace which I obtained yesterday; I have come right away to pay my debt by giving fifteen shillings for the poor."

———

THE YELLOW HOUSE
VISITS TO PRISONERS
1836

The "Yellow House", as it has been called in the annals of the community on account of its color, was located at the corner of Saint Catherine and Saint Christopher Streets. It was a modest two story wooden building, sixty feet in length by forty in width, situated close to Saint James Cathedral and the episcopal palace. Thanks to these neighbors, the work for aged and infirm women was to receive a strong and beneficial impetus through the kind solicitude of the Bishop and because of this, it would soon become the cradle of the Institute.

Emilie Gamelin lost no time in having the most urgent repairs done, to which there was very generous help from the donor. As soon as the renovations were complete, she moved into the new quarters accompanied by Miss Durand and twenty-four elderly ladies from the refuge on Saint Philippe Street. It was the 3rd of May 1836.

The seminary also came to her aid through the intervention of Father Saint Pierre, whose sympathy and kindness towards Mrs. Gamelin and her home for the aged never wavered. Emilie was given the task of distributing the alms that the seminary gave to the underprivileged of the area with the understanding that she could keep a certain amount of the money for her house.

Always ready to lighten misfortune and ease suffering, Mrs. Gamelin did not confine her devotedness and zeal to the service of the poor in her own refuge and immediate neighborhood. The insurrection of 1837 gave her the opportunity of proving the far-reaching nature of her charity.

The Montreal prison was overflowing with political prisoners, many of whom belonged to prominent families. They were strictly forbidden to communicate with their wives and children, which meant cruel suffering for all of them and intensified the anguish and uncertainty of their situation.

Mrs. Gamelin, touched by their misfortune, did all she could to help them. Filled with compassion she lovingly visited the prisoners encouraging them so that they did not lose their faith or hope.

Thanks to the esteem in which she was held and the influence, which she enjoyed, she obtained from the prison authorities a general permission to visit the prisoners as often as she wished and to bring them such help as she considered necessary.

Emilie made good use of this authorization. Every day accompanied by one of the ladies of charity, very often Mrs. Gauvin, Emilie, a basket of provisions on her arm would enter the dreary building. When she went by, the English soldiers would present arms, in response to her greeting.

The news of this favor, which had been granted to Mrs. Gamelin, quickly spread throughout the countryside. Soon the relatives and friends of the prisoners confided to her their messages, letters and gifts. Emilie accepted this additional service with joy. It was her ministry of compassion and kindness, which paved the way for the conversion of many souls. She became known throughout the city as the Angel of Prisoners.[5]

———

We ate bread only once a day. Our usual fare consisted of pea soup, lard and potatoes. During Lent and on days of abstinence, we had pea soup and apple pie without bread or butter. We never bought tea or coffee, but we sent someone to the village to pick up tealeaves, which had already been used. One day, a gentleman gave the orphans fifty cents to buy taffy. Sister superior, who had no more bread to give them, asked the children, which they would prefer, bread or taffy. "Oh! Bread, bread!" cried the children in unison, because bread was for them what sweets are to the children of the rich.

———

5. *Idem*, pages 36 to 40.

THE BIRTH OF A WORK
1841

Soon after his return from Europe on October 16, 1841, Bishop Bourget assembled the ladies of the new association in the little oratory of the refuge, where he blessed them and encouraged them in their labors. After singing a few hymns together, the good Bishop addressed the little gathering with a discourse full of warmth and kindness, which seemed to come from a heart overflowing with charity. Recalling the beautiful words of Saint Lawrence to the Roman proconsul, he spoke to them of the real treasure that the Church has in the poor, the disabled and the sick. The persons that they were assisting and of whom they had become the guardians were the suffering body of Christ whose wounds they dressed and whose sorrow they relieved.

Saint Vincent de Paul, no doubt, would have spoken in the same way to the ladies in Paris, France who were associated with his works of charity. Just as they were moved by the inspiring words of St. Vincent, the ladies of Montreal, were touched by the words of Bishop Bourget, and felt encouraged to continue with enthusiasm this generous work.

Providence Asile. The center part was built in 1842-1843;
the right wing in 1845 and the left wing in 1858. It was
demolished in December 1963 to create the place for the
Metro Station of Berri-De Montigny (Berri-UQAM)

Bishop Bourget, gave them hope for the future of the
humble refuge, which they had taken under their care. During the regular meeting, over which he presided following
the religious ceremony in the oratory, he told them about his
plan of bringing the Daughters of Charity of Saint Vincent
de Paul to his episcopal city to take charge of the refuge. In
his recent visit to Paris, their Superior General had agreed to
his request.

The next day the women decided to purchase a piece of
land for the construction of a new refuge. Thanks to the
generosity of the husband of one of the ladies, Paul Joseph
Lacroix and of his sister, Louise Lacroix, who advanced them

the necessary funds, they became the owners of a splendid terrain covered with vines and fruit trees. It measured 56,000 feet in surface area and adjoined the grounds of the bishop's palace, extending to a point just opposite the Yellow House.

Even the children were caught up by the fervor of zeal. A future Archbishop of Montreal, Charles Edward Fabre, then only twelve years old, helped, with all the care and attention possible for his age, in the bazaars in which his mother took a very active part for the benefit of the refuge.

Then there was the charming incident of four little girls of Montreal who, all on their own, organized a bazaar in favor of the refuge. Their names deserve to be mentioned: Alida Bourret, Eleonore Simpson, Virginie Roy, and Marie Louise Leprohon. The oldest was nine years old and the youngest seven.

It was vacation time. These dear children asked permission from their mothers to use the time to work for the poor. Needless to say, their mothers readily consented and the girls immediately set to work making dresses for dolls. At the end of three weeks they asked Mrs. Bourret, Alida's mother and the wife of the mayor of Montreal, to let them use her drawing room so that the bazaar might be held there under her patronage. It was a great success, lasting only one evening and all of the articles were sold.

The next day, Mrs. Bourret presented these children to the Bishop and they placed about ten louis in his hands. They addressed him in words of touching simplicity, "Your Grace, we have had a great bazaar and we bring you the proceeds. If you wish you can give them to the Providence refuge which you are building for Mrs. Gamelin's poor people."

The Spirit of God, which at all times governs and animates the Church, had decided to raise up at that time, along with the Sisters of Jeanne Mance and the daughters of Marguerite Bourgeoys and of Marguerite Marie Dufrost de la Jemmerais, a new community, called to provide for new needs, to relieve other sufferings, and thus to complete the organization of religious life in the city of Montreal.[6]

—⁓⁓—

Another day, the cash on hand amounted to a few cents. The Sisters and the poor assisted at Mass in honor of Saint Joseph, begging him to come to their aid. Around nine o'clock, a stranger rang the doorbell and said: "I am a traveler. I was in danger of death, and I promised that if I were spared, I would give an offering for the poor. I am happy to keep my promise by giving alms for your house." He gave the sister two louis.

—⁓⁓—

---

6. *Idem*, pages 52 to 73.

THE SISTERS OF CHARITY
OF PROVIDENCE
1843

During the month of February 1843, Bishop Bourget summoned the ladies of charity to a special meeting to announce an unexpected event, which was destined to give their work a new direction and to effect a radical change in the life of Emilie Gamelin.

The Bishop had just received a letter from Father Timon, superior of the Daughters of Saint Vincent de Paul in the United States, informing him, that it was impossible, for the moment to accept the refuge in Montreal. The reason for the refusal was the lack of personnel due to the almost simultaneous foundation of two new houses, one in Algeria and the other in Rome. This was a heavy blow to the hopes of the women and a trial that could have disheartened them, slowed their activity and abated the ardor of their zeal.

It was not, however, enough to shake the constancy of the Bishop or to weaken his confidence in Providence, which he felt would never fail him in an undertaking that had given such bright promise and had enjoyed so successful a beginning.

It was almost impossible for him to apply to another French community. First of all, the choice of such a community, the uncertainty as to its answer, and the time involved in the necessary correspondence would place serious obstacles in the way, at a time when enthusiasm for the work was at its height. Furthermore, the construction of the refuge was rapidly approaching completion, and they needed to be able to count on someone who would take charge.

Any delay or uncertainty would, in fact, constitute a grave menace to the success of the work.

Bishop Bourget, after much prayer and reflection, decided upon a course of action which, although it offered risks and inconveniences, seemed to be the wisest and safest. He resolved to found a diocesan congregation of Sisters of Charity.

The preceding year, having just celebrated Mass in the cathedral of Chartres in France, Bishop Bourget was praying that the Daughters of Charity would establish a community in Montreal, when an unknown person approached offering him the gift of seven rosaries of Our Lady of Seven Dolors.

Later on, Bishop Bourget would give these seven rosaries to the first seven professed religious in the newly founded community, among whom would be counted Emilie Gamelin. It would seem that God wished to sanction, in a mysterious way, the devotion which the new community would have to the sorrows of the Mother of Jesus.

The first religious clothing took place in the humble oratory of the Yellow House, on March 25, 1843. The seven postulants received the religious habit from the hands of Bishop Bourget who, inspired by the liturgy of the day and with deep emotion, addressed them with the following words:

"As the Archangel Gabriel announced to Mary the mystery of the incarnation, so do I announce to you, in the name of the Church, that you are charged with the care of the poor, becoming for them true mothers."

The ceremony of religious clothing made a deep impression on Emilie Gamelin. Her aspirations towards religious life and the desire, which had been part of her for some time now, took on new force. Upon seeing these young women respond to this first call to consecrate themselves to the service of the poor, in the house that she had opened and to which she had already given the best part of her heart and of her life, she felt moved to do the same.

On July 8, 1843, when one of the novices put aside the habit having decided to return home, Mrs. Gamelin could no longer resist. She went immediately to her spiritual director and with tears begged him to allow her to take the place of the one that had just left. Canon Prince received this request coldly and advised her to put aside all thought of religious life, in which he did not yet see the will of God for her. As usual, she submitted without reply, however, she continued to pray and soon afterwards her last hesitations vanished and she took her decision.

Before accepting her desire to begin the novitiate though, Bishop Bourget and Canon Prince decided that Mrs. Gamelin should go to the United States in order to visit some of the houses of charity there, especially those of the Daughters of Saint Vincent de Paul in New York and Baltimore. Thus, she would be able to render greater service to the community of which she was to be a part and for which she would be designated as superior.

A few months before her departure, she had directed the installation of the personnel of the refuge in their new quarters, which then comprised a chapel and two lateral wings. On May 18th Bishop Bourget blessed the wards for the disabled elderly ladies and on the 24th, the feast of Our Lady of Good Help, Mrs. Gamelin and the novices left the Yellow House, which had witnessed so many acts of charity, devotedness, and self-sacrifice. It was farewell to the cradle of the community the memory of which has always remained so dear.

The blessing of the chapel and of the altar took place on the 21st of August. Bishop Phelan, coadjutor bishop of Kingston, Ontario officiated at the ceremony at which were present Bishop Bourget of Montreal, Bishop Signay of Québec, Bishop Gaulin of Kingston and Bishop Power of Toronto. This gathering of prelates was an eloquent witness to the importance with which the Canadian episcopate regarded the new foundation.

Towards the end of August 1844, the house received a gift from Canon Hudon, the vicar general, who was in Europe at the time. It was a statue of Our Lady of Seven Dolors, which Canon Hudon had sent to Mrs. Gamelin. The statue was placed in the niche over the arch, where it replaced the one of the Immaculate Conception, which was transferred to the facade. It would be before this statue of Our Lady of Seven Dolors that the sister foundresses, and so many sisters after them, would pronounce their religious profession.

On the 11th of September, Mrs. Gamelin left for the United States in the company of Mr. Paul Joseph Lacroix and her friends, Mrs. Nolan and Mrs. Gauvin.

Mrs. Gamelin returned to Montreal on October 6, 1843 following an absence of twenty days. Two days later on October 8th, Mrs. Gamelin set aside her secular attire to don the poor and humble habit of the Sisters of Charity of Providence. She was then forty-three years old.[7]

7. *Idem*, pages 73 to 94.

THE WORK MAKES GREAT STRIDES
1844

Canon Prince showed great devotion and unfailing kind ness towards his spiritual daughters; but he was at the same time firm, austere and inflexible in his relationship with them and did not spare them trials. The sisters, filled with emotion, would recall the numerous penances, humiliations and continual renunciation, which he imposed on them and especially upon Sister Gamelin the eldest novice.

Since being widowed, Emilie had directed the course of her own life, which her means had made relatively easy. Even when her time and energy were devoted to works of piety and charity, she enjoyed complete control of her liberty. From the moment of her entrance into the novitiate however she found herself subjected to a rigorous rule, which from morning till night curtailed her freedom and imposed demands on her that were altogether foreign to her previous way of life.

She had to live the common life, severe and poor as it was, with no alleviation or exemptions. She had to become a child again, to bear with differences of taste and character, to practice charity and gentleness in the midst of contradictions; in a word, she had to perform daily acts of self-denial and mortification of which only God knew the number and the merit.

Never-the-less this change did not make a dent in her character, she retained all of the vivacity that she needed to give energy to her life, to stir up the fire of zeal. Her natural pride became a grave and unaffected dignity. Her sensitivity was channeled into tender and compassionate concern for the unfortunate, and loving devotion to our Mother of Sorrows, into whose heart she poured out her own sorrow and distress.

Bishop Bourget shared with Canon Prince the difficult and delicate task of forming the novices in the spirit and virtues of their new state of life. Besides the spiritual exercises given them each day by Canon Prince, Bishop Bourget personally presided over their spiritual reading and explained to them the rule of Saint Vincent de Paul, which was to be that of the community. As early as five o'clock in the morning, he presided over their meditation in order to initiate them into the Ignatian method of prayer and he gave them frequent spiritual conferences. Profoundly convinced that the edifice of their perfection must be built on solid foundations, he spared himself no pains to form them in the virtues essential to their state: love of God, zeal for the glory of God, the service of their neighbor, humility and self-denial. His counsels, his letters, both personal and official, are monuments to his devoted zeal but at the same time, models of that gentle yet strong direction which he knew would most effectively dispose souls towards the practice of perfection.

Under his influence, the novices more and more convinced of their vocation, longed for the moment of their religious profession. Bishop Bourget preached the preparatory retreat for the great day.

The ceremony of religious profession took place on March 29, 1844, a memorable date in the annals of the Institute because it marked the beginning of the community and assured its stability. How many hopes were realized on that day! How many doubts were set to rest! How many fears were dispelled! How many so called follies were transformed into wisdom! The anguish and the difficulties of the beginnings were forgotten. The work of Providence was manifest and the designs of God's goodness and mercy triumphed.

The community was organized and the purpose of the Institute officially defined. In addition to the exterior works of charity, forty-two disabled persons at the refuge enjoyed the care and attention of these first Sisters who had to multiply themselves to respond to their needs. Mother Gamelin gave herself no rest. Her beloved asylum was still sparsely furnished. There were barely enough chairs for each sister to sit down after a day of fatiguing work. During the day they seldom enjoyed the luxury of sitting down to rest although the hour for rising was half past four every morning.

Their poverty was very great, their food extremely frugal. It is difficult to understand how these sisters, in the midst of such privation could have accomplished the amount of work which they took upon themselves.

Faced with the demands of an administration that was becoming more complicated each day, Mother Gamelin drew constantly from her deep faith in Providence. She had a thousand ingenious ways of calming anxiety and restoring confidence. One day, the sister cook came to tell her that there was nothing for dinner. "Do not fear, my daughter," she said calmly, "Providence will not fail to send us our dinner. Come with me, and let us sing to show that we are not at all anxious," and she led the way to the elderly women's ward. On seeing their mother approaching, they gathered around her as they always did. "There is a favor I want to obtain from Providence, and I would like you to join me in singing our beautiful hymn." The dear elderly women, at once all attention, mingled their trembling voices with that of Mother Gamelin and her companion and sang the following hymn with full voice:

O Providence, most gentle,[8]
Whose bounteous hands bestow,
Upon us in abundance
All good things here below,
Acknowledging the Author
Of all these gifts divine,
Ourselves and all that's ours,
To Him we should resign.

If riches He outpoureth
On springtime's early flower,
With largesses enriching
The grass that lasts an hour;
More fully He bestoweth
On man beloved His aid;
That being whom His wisdom
To His own image made.

If God who loves us dearly
His care doth not disdain
To sparrows in the tree tops,
Their little lives sustain,

---

8. I found this expression "Gentle Providence" in the Dialogues of St. Catherine of Sienna, quoted in the "Liturgy of the Hours" of Saturday of the 30th week in Ordinary Time. Holiness is always the same, over time and space.

The Author of all nature
Shall He then man forget,
The noblest of the creatures,
That He hath fashioned yet?[9]

On leaving the room, Mother Gamelin went to the kitchen where she found some leftovers from the previous meal, hardly enough for five or six people. "Warm it up", she said, smiling at the sister cook, "and you will see that dinner can be served". In fact, dinner was served to the whole house, the dishes on each table were filled, and there was some left over when the meal was ended. The treasurer of the time and those who succeeded her relate that this miracle of Providence was often repeated and that provisions which should have run out in a week lasted for months without seeming to diminish.

Singing was one of Mother Gamelin's spiritual resources. When she found herself in financial difficulty, she sang and had her sisters sing their favorite hymn "O Providence Most Gentle". If any shade of sadness hovered over the recreation of the community, she immediately began to sing:

Enjoy, O fervent souls,
Your happiness enjoy.

The others caught up the melody with enthusiasm and the sadness was quickly dispelled.

There are hymns that die out and others that live on. We have found here one of Mother Gamelin's favorite songs, which has always been held in esteem in the community.

---

9. *La femme au cœur attentif*, Mère Gamelin, par Eugène Nadeau, O.M.I., p. 307.

It prolonged the tremulous voices of the elderly women, which Mother Gamelin loved to make vibrate, in the early days of the foundation, when her protegees needed to be reassured, or when it was necessary to send an urgent appeal for the poor to our Provident God.

Bishop Bourget appreciated this spirit of joyful melody in the exercise of charity. Doubtless he was alluding to it in the following lines dedicated to Mother Gamelin after her death in 1851. "It was good to see her in the community rooms, surrounded by her dear elderly ladies, whose cheerful serenity gave proof that in the presence of Mother Gamelin they forgot their suffering. Having enjoyed the privilege of frequently assisting at this touching scene, it is with profound emotion that I give testimony to this happy memory of Mother Gamelin. These have remained engraved in my soul, and now that she is no longer among us they become more vivid than ever…" (Mélanges Religieux, October 10, 1851).

The hymn, "O Providence Most Gentle" (sung to the music of *Partant pour la Syrie*) was published with a collection of hymns found in Québec in 1819, under the signature of Father Jean Denis Daulé.

In Montreal, Mother Gamelin made it immortal.

Mother Gamelin was very fond of music and singing and, for a long time, she herself directed the choir of the house. At that time, they had no musical instruments. The Sisters sang in the first gallery of the chapel, often on their knees, or like Saint Teresa and her companions sitting on their heels. Since they were not very numerous, all the Sisters joined in the singing. Bishop Bourget encouraged their pious emulation. "Sing", he said to them, "sing in the sanctuary, imitate the soft cry of doves. Let your favorite hymn be the "Stabat Mater". Your simple hymns your reverent canticles may convert souls that the finest sermons could not touch."[10]

———

10. *Idem*, pages 94 to 112.

A MONTH OF BLESSINGS
May 1844

May of 1844 was a month of blessings for the little community. The Blessed Mother granted favors with great generosity and the sisters intensified their homage of respect and gratitude towards her. Mother Gamelin wanted the loveliest flowers from the garden to adorn the altar of Mary each day. "May the perfume of those flowers", she said, "heal the wounds of her heart pierced by so many swords of sorrow."

Every evening the little family gathered in the humble chapel to sing their most beautiful hymns. However, the best offering that was made to Our Blessed Mother was the work on behalf of orphan girls, which was inaugurated on the first day of that month.

Mother Gamelin's compassionate heart was moved with pity upon seeing the great number of poor girls left without shelter or protection following the death of their parents. In their isolation, these children were exposed to all sorts of dangers. The limited resources of the asylum did not seem to allow for the opening of an orphanage. Nevertheless, the tireless zeal of Mother Gamelin enabled her to find the necessary means. She convened the Ladies of Charity to a special meeting. There she spoke to them with so much warmth and feeling on behalf of these poor children, whose mothers in many instances had died in her arms, that the ladies decided without hesitation to accept them. They immediately prepared to receive a dozen orphans in a room of the asylum that was set aside for them, and in order to operate the work they pledged to pay from ten to fifteen shillings a month for their board and lodging.

So not only was the work accepted in principle, but the work itself was founded, to the great joy of Mother Gamelin.

It was to obtain additional resources for this new work that Mother Gamelin, on September 10, 1844, founded the project of lady boarders. As well, various departments were opened where the sisters made cassocks and church ornaments, candles and hosts, together with soap making and weaving. Since the days were not long enough to accomplish all the work a part of the night had to be given to it. Frequently, after long vigils at the bedside of the sick poor in an overheated and foul atmosphere, the sisters went cheerfully back to their work in the morning, having taken very little rest. This makes us realize that it is due to the hard work of these first valiant sisters that we owe the blessings and the prosperity that the institute enjoys today.

Mother Gamelin was always deeply grateful towards all the benefactors of the house. She spoke of them with deep respect mingled with grateful affection. Prayers were said every day for their intentions, and it was her desire that the sisters remain faithful to their memory. She often and earnestly recommended to the sisters that they should be very cordial in thanking anyone from whom they received even the least offering or the smallest alms.

The ladies of charity, who had given such tremendous help in the foundation of the work, could always count on her special affection and thoughtful concern. As early as the 15th of November 1843, she organized for them a three-day retreat, preached by Bishop Bourget, in the new chapel.

In September of the following year, she organized a second retreat, preached by Fathers Léonard, Lagier, and Guigues, of the Congregation of the Oblates of Mary Immaculate.[11] Mother Gamelin's extensive influence attracted to these retreats a large number of women and young girls. Some of them stayed overnight at the asylum during those days in order to enjoy a more prayerful atmosphere.

The day of the closing of the retreats was a day of special celebration for the sisters. The ladies themselves served a gala dinner for the elderly women and the orphans, spending most of the day with them to entertain and amuse them. They would leave in the evening following Benediction of the Blessed Sacrament, leaving a sense of sweetness and joy in the hearts of all these people who were deprived of the intimate affection and happiness of family life. At the same time, filled with the love of God, they had rekindled their own tenderness and compassion towards their neighbor.

These festivals organized for the poor were a source of great happiness to Mother Gamelin. She rejoiced in the pleasure reflected in the faces of her dear old people whom she loved so much.

During the course of the year 1845, the community would experience two trials. The first was the departure of Canon

---

11. Father Eugène Guigues was consecrated first Bishop of Ottawa, July 30, 1848.

Prince, chaplain of the asylum. Named on July 5th as coadjutor Bishop of Bishop Bourget, he was obliged to give up his duties as chaplain on the 10th of November. However, since he was still the superior of the house, he continued to maintain the strong and valuable ties which his devotedness and wisdom had created. Canon Alexis-Frederic Truteau succeeded him as chaplain.

The second trial was much more serious. In the month of October, a fire completely destroyed the Yellow House. The Sisters, to their great sorrow, watched the flames devour that first refuge, the true cradle of the Community, where they had labored with such fervor. They could not restrain their tears at the loss of this house, which had sheltered them during the first days of their religious life and that had harbored the hopes and first fruits of the work of their beloved Foundress.[12]

One day, Mother Gamelin said to Mr. Jean Bruneau, "As people grow older, they become more sensitive to the cold. Last night I went to see our elderly ladies and I found several of them suffering from the cold." The kind gentleman understood and that same day, he sent her a few dozen warm woolen blankets.

---

12. *Idem*, pages 112 to 119.

GROWTH IN SUFFERING
1845

Mother Gamelin was frequently concerned with the many financial problems resulting from the various works she had undertaken.

The poor came to her from all over. Many people forget that once the houses of charity are built, they are not self-supporting. They have to be heated, maintained, kept in repair. The poor whom they shelter must be fed, clothed, and cared for when they are sick. Their operation requires continual resources.

The asylum was hardly completed, built through the generosity of the citizens of Montreal, when requests to take persons began to arrive from various parishes of the diocese and even from neighboring dioceses.

For the compassionate heart of Mother Gamelin, it was very difficult to be obliged to close the door to so many poor elderly women who were abandoned by their impoverished families and who had nowhere to go. They needed a home, someplace where they might receive even the most elementary care during the last days of a life that had been filled with privation and hard work. She confided her sorrow and her concerns to her companions and to the ladies of charity, insisting that at all costs they needed to enlarge the house and to do so without delay. The Bishop approved of her project.

The work was begun at once and the construction advanced with great enthusiasm. By the following autumn the elderly women and the orphan girls were able to take possession of their new, spacious and well-lighted quarters.

Mother Gamelin rejoiced at anything that increased the well being of her elderly and infirm women, for whom she felt a truly maternal tenderness. Her faith made her see in them the suffering members of Christ and inspired in her a profound respect for them, which she manifested even at their death. Carrying a lighted candle, she always accompanied their mortal remains to the door of the asylum, when they left for their last resting-place.

This respect, she exacted from everybody in the house. One day she reprimanded a novice, who in her presence had called one of the elderly women, "old So and So". "Can you not refer to her as Mrs.?...." she observed. When the novice knelt down to ask pardon, she said, "Go to the chapel and ask pardon of Our Lord for it is He whom you have offended in the person of that poor woman".

Every day, no matter what her concerns might be, she visited the wards of the sick and infirm. She quieted their little annoyances and exhorted them to endure their troubles patiently while awaiting that blessed reward which their advanced years permitted them to see so near at hand. It was when she was with them that her great kindness and charity towards those who are suffering or unfortunate in any way, could best be observed. To render the smallest and most distasteful services was for her a joy, which was evident in her whole person. One would have believed that it was a mother caring for her own children.

She loved to pray with them and to make the Stations of the Cross in their wards. On Sunday she assembled everyone in the house and she explained the catechism. Eloquent in speech, she became even more so when speaking on spiritual topics. It would seem that her voice expressed all the eagerness and outpouring of her heart. The hour of instruction, therefore, was always eagerly awaited and sincerely enjoyed. She pointed out their duties, gave maternal advice, indicated any infractions of the Rule committed during the week and then distributed little rewards to the orphans. If the pictures and medals had run out, she gave them a small candy in an envelope that had been addressed with the name of Mother Gamelin. Her name on the envelope seemed to enhance the taste of the contents.

What can be said of the wonderful gift she possessed for assisting the dying in their final hours. The sick wanted to be assured in advance that she would be present during their last hours where she would enliven their faith and deepen their confidence in the merits of the passion of Our Lord. To them she seemed to hold in her hands the key to heaven, which would open wide its doors to receive them. According to the testimony of the sisters of that time, it was very touching to hear her speak to the dying of the infinite mercy of God. To listen as she recited the liturgical prayers recommending the departing soul to God, giving back to the Creator and Redeemer those whom Providence had entrusted to her and for whom she never ceased to pray. The sisters have preserved these memories which allow us to admire the profound sense of faith and unfailing hope of Mother Gamelin in a ministry that requires so much commitment and dedication.

On Holy Thursday, Mother Gamelin washed the feet of twelve elderly women in memory of the great act of humility of Our Savior. She dried them with her own hands and kissed them respectfully, thus renewing, for the edification of the sisters, this great lesson which Our Lord gave to the apostles on the true nature and duties of Christian authority.

The charity of Mother Gamelin was not confined solely to the poor of her asylum; as she continued to devote herself to the other poor just as before. The first novices, as soon as they were clothed with the religious habit, accompanied her on the visits she had for many years made to the poor of the city. Since 1828, Emilie Gamelin had not allowed a day to pass without visiting some of these needy people. She was always ready to console them in their troubles, providing for both their spiritual and temporal needs.

The soup kitchen was another scene of her active charity. From the time of the opening of the little refuge in the Yellow House, she distributed soup and other food to all those who came.

From the beginning, Bishop Bourget had placed the institute under the special protection of Our Lady of Seven Dolors. In his written instructions, he often insisted on the importance and the value of this devotion as well as that of the Passion of Our Lord.

The devotion to Our Lady of Seven Dolors is essential to your institute.

Our Lord, in His mercy, has deigned to bring you together in community under the protection of Mary desolate. For this reason God, in loving Providence, willed that the seven foundresses of this new community would take the religious habit on March 25. This is the day that commemorates the incarnation of Our Lord in the womb of His Blessed Mother and the day, according to some authorities, that He died on Calvary before the eyes of His blessed Mother.

In this way, you have been born to religious life on Calvary, near the Cross, at the feet of Jesus Christ dying, and in the heart of Mary pierced with the seven swords of sorrow, when all nature was in mourning for the death of its creator. You are then, children of the sorrows of Mary and are therefore obliged to spread, whenever possible, this salutary devotion, for it is the cornerstone upon which rests the edifice of your Community.

In his eagerness to imprint this beautiful devotion ever more deeply in the hearts of the sisters, he wrote to them in the following terms:

Be completely filled with the truth that you were born to religious life at the foot of the cross and in the heart of Our Mother of Sorrows. As well, it is to the precious blood of Jesus and the bitter tears of Mary that you owe your astonishing growth in so short a time. May the passion of Our Lord Jesus Christ be for you a divine strength that serves as a rampart to defend and protect you. May His death obtain eternal glory for you and enable you to live, in the faithful practice of all the religious virtues.

May the Holy Cross preserve this community, founded in our own day to celebrate the mysteries of Calvary and to console our Mother of Sorrows, by relieving the miseries which afflict humanity.

He even went so far as to say, "The devotion to Our Mother of Sorrows is the devotion proper to your humble institute. The institute was born and grew up with it and it always has been and always will be its strength. If this devotion were to disappear the institute will disappear with it."

During his trips to Rome, Bishop Bourget had discovered this devotion in the Order of the Servites of Mary. Thus on July 7, 1855 he was admitted to the Third Order of the Servites of Mary, at their General House of Saint Marcel in Rome.[13]

All that we have learned up to now about Mother Gamelin, shows to what extent she was penetrated with the virtues and the spirit that Bishop Bourget tried so hard to impart to these spiritual daughters. She was a true model of life for them and it can be affirmed that, in practice, she had begun her novitiate long before she ever decided to wear the religious habit.

13. Archives of the Order, 1855.

BRANCHING OUT
1846

Mother Gamelin founded her first mission outside of Montreal about five miles from the city, in the village of Longue Pointe, located on the banks of the Saint Lawrence River. We do not know if Mother Gamelin already foresaw the advantages that such a foundation would have for the future of the congregation and for the works of charity which the community would later undertake. Certainly, we do not know what she was thinking, but if she did have such foresight, it was justified because two of the most important works originated there, the work with deaf persons and that for the mentally ill.

In the spring of 1846, Mother Gamelin installed two of her Sisters in the little house on the farm of Saint Isidore, where they opened an elementary school.

The following year Mother Gamelin had them build an extension on the house, as it was now too small for their needs.

In 1852, the sisters opened at Longue Pointe a hospice for the mentally ill on the farm at Saint Isidore. The pupils had been moved to a larger stone house, forty by thirty feet in size, bought with all its dependencies on a large piece of land, close to the parish church.

At the Saint Isidore farm, the classrooms were converted into wards and seventeen mentally ill persons were moved in. Of this number eight came from the asylum, where Mother Gamelin, in November of 1845, had set aside for them a small house located within the enclosure of the garden. Ever since she had adopted Dodais, following the death of her husband, Mother Gamelin had always taken a special interest in mentally ill persons. God blessed this work as well as all the others that she undertook.

That same year, the Saint Isidore farm opened its doors to aged and sick priests. In July 1845, Mother Gamelin had opened a refuge for priests, in a house that belonged to Judge Pike, very near the asylum, at the corner of Mignone and St. Hubert Streets. She had bought the house for this purpose and it was known as Saint Joseph Hospice.

On the 8th of July 1852, a fire destroyed the entire suburb of Saint Lawrence and a part of the Quebec suburb. The Providence asylum and the Saint Joseph Hospice, though the latter was of wood, were saved from the disaster by a singular protection of Heaven. Right beside them, the cathedral and the Bishop's palace were reduced to ashes. Fourteen hundred houses were destroyed and nearly nine thousand persons were left homeless.

The Asylum opened its doors to a multitude of these unfortunate people. All the rooms, even the chapel, were converted into dormitories, where nothing was heard but sighs and lamentations.

The priests of the Saint Joseph Hospice touched by the sad plight of their Bishop and the clergy of his household spontaneously offered him their dwelling, which became the Bishop's residence. The chapel of the Asylum served as the fourth cathedral of Montreal.[14] The priests of the Hospice confided to the Sisters of Providence the care of finding them another residence.

The Sisters managed to find accommodations for them at the Saint Isidore farm, where they spent the next three years, until the temporary cathedral and the Bishop's palace had been built in the suburb of St. Antoine. In the meantime, the chapel of the Asylum was used for public religious worship and as well, the Bishop officiated at all pontifical ceremonies there.

Almost simultaneously with the establishment of the Saint Isidore house at Longue Pointe, Mother Gamelin opened a house in Laprairie at the request of the pastor, Jesuit Father Tellier. The Association of the Ladies of Charity, which had been organized in that parish in the year 1842, also earnestly entreated Mother Gamelin to come. This appeal awakened a ready response in the heart of Mother Gamelin because the new foundation was established, in many respects, under the same circumstances as that of Montreal. There, also, a society of ladies had taken the initiative in visiting and caring for the poor.

They had even rented a house to shelter those among them who had no decent dwelling. The ladies turned the house over to Mother Gamelin on the 15th of May 1846. At that time, it sheltered eight elderly and handicapped women, who had been placed under the care of a pious lady named Emmélie Denaud.

The arrival of the Sisters was a source of great joy to the poor families of the village. Mother Gamelin spent some

---

14. Cf. *Le diocèse de Montréal à la fin du dix-neuvième siècle*, Eusèbe Sénécal, et Cie. Montréal, 1900.

days there with the sisters to make the beginnings of their new life a little easier. She gave special attention to the preparation of the little oratory, which was soon to receive the Blessed Sacrament whose Presence is the great support and the principal consolation of religious life.

The Sisters had the joy of participating in the first Mass in their oratory on the 26th of May. It was celebrated by Bishop Prince, who immediately after Mass assembled the Ladies of Charity, congratulated them on the work already accomplished, and strongly exhorted them to give the sisters the full support of their zeal and devotedness.

A few days later, Bishop Bourget himself came to bring to the religious and the ladies the powerful encouragement of his presence and his words. He promised the women that a Mass would be offered for their intentions on Monday of each week, during which an instruction would be given by one of the Jesuit Fathers of the parish.

In spite of the meager resources of the house, which was completely dependent on public charity, the foundation, never-the-less began under the happiest of circumstances. A terrible trial, however, threatened to destroy that fortunate beginning.

The night of August 5th, a portion of the village was destroyed by fire. More than three hundred houses, the rectory and a part of the Hospice went up in flames. The fire stopped at the church.

The Sisters and the fourteen poor and handicapped women took refuge on the riverbank. There Mother Gamelin found them the following morning when, upon hearing the sad news, she hurried to the scene. They were surrounded by hundreds of homeless and unfortunate people, gathered around the articles of furniture and clothing that they had managed to save from the disaster.

After offering comfort and encouragement with her usual kindness and compassion, Mother Gamelin immediately returned to the Asylum taking with her the fourteen aged women from the Hospice. The Sisters found refuge with the sisters of the Congregation of Notre Dame.

Mother Gamelin came back frequently with Sister Caron to give to these families in distress whatever assistance was most urgently needed. Meanwhile, relief committees were being organized in the city and in the neighboring countryside to aid the victims of the fire and the sisters were placed in charge of the distribution of the money, food, and clothing. Immediately, Mother Gamelin, assisted by Sister Caron, presided at the first distribution.

When the most necessary repairs had been made, the sisters were able to return to their house on the 24th of September and their poor people followed them in the month of November.

Nevertheless, the poverty of the house continued to be extreme and at times even essential things were wanting. Mother Gamelin was on the point of recalling her sisters but yielded to their entreaties to remain with the poor whom they did not want to abandon. To the pleas of the sisters were added those of Father Tellier and the Ladies of Charity. They had set to work collecting articles and holding bazaars not only to defray the cost of repairs necessitated by the fire, but also to secure for the sisters the title of ownership of the house for which they were paying an annual rent of 19 louis.

The Ladies succeeded in obtaining from the relief committee a donation of 50 louis and as well Father Tellier traveled to Quebec to solicit alms. His efforts were successful and he brought back the sum of 147 louis which made possible the acquisition of the property, although there still remained a debt of 400 louis.

This was Father Tellier's last act of zeal and devotedness in favor of the foundation in which he had played so considerable a part. On The 7th of December of that year Reverend Father Mainguy replaced him as the pastor of Laprairie.

Less than a year later, on October 16, 1847, Mother Gamelin was obliged to open a ward for orphans in that same mission. Many poor, abandoned children could find no place in other charitable institutions. To provide for the needs of these new boarders, the sisters took upon themselves an increase of work, even going so far as to depend on the food that was left over from the meals for the poor. Here was another trait that was a characteristic of the foundation of the Sisters of Providence.

We should also note that Mother Gamelin had a very special place in her heart for the foreign missions. We can believe that if the year following her death, a group of sisters were sent to Oregon, to establish a new mission in 1852, it was due in large part to her hopes and prayers.[15]

—⁓—

Everywhere she recommended to the sisters love for the poor, union, mutual charity and confidence in God. "Fear nothing," she often repeated, "as long as you are surrounded by the poor, Providence will be your help as well as your faithful treasurer. Believe me, you will lack nothing."

—⁓—

15. *Idem*, pages 122 to 140.

THE YEAR OF THE IRISH
AND THE TYPHUS
1847

We now touch upon a very sad period in the history of Montreal. The Community of Providence will have the mission of bringing consolation to the victims of this terrible tragedy. The passing years can never erase nor allow to be overlooked the dedication of the sisters during this time.

In 1847, the twofold scourge of typhus and famine decimated Ireland. The people were dying by the thousands. The houses were deserted and many who attempted to escape the scourge, died on the roads.

Faced with such extreme misery, a great many Irish people hoped to find in America a second homeland, where they could survive and freely practice their religion. England encouraged their immigration to Canada.

A large number of ships were chartered. Hundreds of unfortunate people, who were already weakened by misery or ill with disease, rushed onto these ships in the hope of finding a new life. But unfortunately the typhoid fever soon broke out on the ships transforming them into floating hospitals. Death spread its ravages among them indiscriminately, separating husband from wife and mother from child. The groans of the dying, the lamentations of mothers and the cries of orphaned children made up a sorrowful concert, but there was no one to bring help on the vast ocean.

When they finally set foot on Canadian soil after that dismal voyage, these unfortunate people once again found themselves faced with death or with the disease, which struck down the small number that up to now had been spared. In this desolation they experienced the charity of the religious sisters who nursed and relieved their suffering and the zeal and piety of the priests who also comforted them and prepared them to return to God.

The Grey Nuns were the first sisters summoned to their aid. At the end of a few weeks thirty of these sisters had contracted the terrible sickness and seven of them died and went to receive the reward of their generous devotion.

It was necessary to replace them by having recourse to another religious community.

Bishop Bourget thought of the Sisters of Providence and went himself to the Asylum to appeal to their devotedness. It was the 24th of June. He assembled the community, which at that time counted nineteen professed sisters, nineteen novices, and fourteen postulants. Explaining the pitiful state of the sick, he asked if any of the religious were willing to sacrifice themselves by risking their lives to care for these unfortunate people. In answer to his question, all stood up and with one voice answered together, "I am ready."

The next morning at half past seven, strengthened by Holy Communion and the blessing of their Bishop, twelve of these brave women, chosen by their superior, got into carriages and were driven to the sheds at Point Saint Charles where a very sad scene awaited them.

Hundreds of sick people, lying on beds of straw, in the throes of suffering were groaning pitifully. Little children were crying inconsolably, still clasped in the arms of their mothers who had died during the night. There were corpses lying everywhere. Women, scarcely able to drag themselves about, sought in that frightful chaos for a husband or for children of whose fate they were ignorant. Such was the dismal picture presented by that scene of suffering.

The Sisters set to work immediately. They first removed the dead and then began to administer to the sick. In this tremendous work, there were none to help except for a few convalescents who assisted with the dying.

The religious of the Hôtel Dieu, in their turn, left their cloister with the Bishop's permission and came for a few days to help the Sisters of Providence in this work of mercy. Working alongside these devoted nurses was Bishop Bourget himself, accompanied by several of the canons and priests of the bishopric, as well as Sulpicians, Jesuits, and diocesan clergy who worked night and day among the sick. They heard confessions, administered the last sacraments and gave all possible encouragement and consolation. Fifty to sixty persons died each day and their bodies, while awaiting burial, were placed in an immense mortuary erected on the bank of the river.

Finally it became possible, thanks to the construction of new sheds, to classify the sick. Men, women, children, and convalescents were separated and distributed among the different sections.

Bishop Bourget suggested that Mother Gamelin should take charge of the orphans, who numbered more than six hundred and occupied two of the temporary hospitals. Deeply touched by the fate of these abandoned children she immediately accepted this work. She secured the use of Mrs. Nolan's house on Saint Catherine Street and sent two sisters there to receive the little boys. Since the house was not furnished, twenty bundles of straw were bought and spread over the floor as sleeping places for these poor little children dressed in rags that scarcely covered them. The girls were confided to the Sisters of the Good Shepherd until a larger house could be found for all of them.

The Sisters of Providence continued to care for the sick at Point St. Charles until the beginning of October. For nearly three months, the sisters of the Congregation of Notre Dame would pick them up in the morning at the Asile and take them back in the evening in large carriages that they had hired for that purpose. The Grey Nuns gave them dinner each day, in their house at Point St. Charles.

For the religious dedicated to this ministry, the annual retreat in July took place there in the midst of their patients. Certainly, Saint Vincent de Paul, the author of their rule, would not have objected to this arrangement.

Among those taking part in that retreat were seven novices soon to be admitted to profession. Where better than in those scenes of charity and devoted sacrifice could they meditate on the life and duties of the Sisters of Providence? They could pronounce their vows as religious with complete confidence as their vocation had been tested. They were converted through their actions into Sisters of Providence.

On the very morning of their profession, at the usual hour, after having embraced their relatives, they returned to the sheds to resume their ministry of service. Twenty-seven of these sisters were eventually stricken with typhus, nine of them received the last sacraments and three of them died.

In view of the sickness and death of these brave nurses, Bishop Bourget was deeply concerned about the danger that threatened the young Institute of Providence. He assembled all the sisters in the oratory and made aloud a vow in the name of all the professed religious, that every Friday in perpetuity there would be seven candles burned in honor of Our Lady of Seven Dolors. This was for the preservation of the Institute, which had been threatened with destruction by the death, or serious illness of the Sisters of Providence who had contracted typhus. The Blessed Mother heard his prayer. The sick sisters were restored to health and after a period of convalescence were able to resume their work.

On the 1st of October, the orphans who had been temporarily installed in Mrs. Nolan's house were able to move to the former convent of the Good Shepherd situated on Beaudry Street, then called Black Horse Street. The new Hospice was placed under the name and protection of Saint Jerome Emilianus. It was large enough to receive, in a separate section, the orphan girls whom the religious of the Good Shepherd had temporarily accepted.

The first superior of this new refuge was Mother Elizabeth, and her companions were Sisters Brigitte and Catherine. An Irish priest, Father Fitzhenry, was placed in charge of religious instruction for all the children.

However, he was not able to continue this ministry for very long and was soon replaced by Mr. Fabre, a seminarian studying theology at the Bishop's Palace. The young ecclesiastic found in this work an interesting field for his zeal. He was deeply devoted to his ministry and had the consolation a few months later of presenting sixty of the children for First Communion and Confirmation.

Since the 11th of July, Mother Gamelin had received 650 orphans at the Saint Jerome Emilianus Hospice. Of that number, 332 eventually died and 188 were placed in homes or were claimed by their families. In March of 1848, there remained 130 children, not counting the 99 children who had stayed in the sheds at Point Saint Charles. At that time, the hospice was entirely dependent on charitable resources, for the government had just withdrawn the modest grant, which it had accorded for a short period.

Bishop Bourget touched by the situation of these unfortunate children and concerned about their future, made a strong appeal in their favor to the people of his diocese.

The number of Irish immigrants who died of typhus in the sheds on Point Saint Charles is estimated at 6000. To perpetuate the memory of that sad event, an enormous block of stone was placed over the graves where the mortal remains of those unfortunate people were buried. The following inscription was engraved thereon:

To preserve from desecration
The remains of 6000 immigrants
Who died of ship fever
A.D. 1847- 48
This stone is erected
By the workmen of Messrs. Peto, Brassey and Betes
Employed in the construction
Of the Victoria Bridge
A. D. 1859[16]

---

16. *Idem*, pages 188 to 200.

DEVELOPMENT OF PROJECTS
1848

After having taken such an important role in the care given to the unfortunate typhus victims, the community was naturally associated with the solemn thanksgiving that Bishop Bourget requested once the epidemic had ceased. Bishop Bourget, during the plague, had made a vow to the Blessed Mother. He had promised to reestablish the pilgrimages to the shrine of Our Lady of Good Help and to promote devotion to her if she would protect the people against the ravages of the disease. The devotion to Our Blessed Mother, that the people once had, had almost completely fallen off through general indifference.

During the period of calm, which followed the days of tribulation, the indefatigable Foundress, Mother Gamelin, planned new charitable undertakings.

One group of persons for whom she felt a particular interest was the domestic servants. These were young women without any protection and thus exposed to the many dangers that isolation in the heart of a big city brings. Emilie Gamelin began by opening a place to receive them and soon formed them into an association under the patronage of Saint Blandine. They obeyed a simple rule, which among other things forbade all luxury in dress and required that they wear clothing suitable to their state. They were trained in domestic work and in the art of cooking. They were exhorted to bear patiently the trials of their situation and to fulfil the duties of their position with devotion and care. These girls had no difficulty finding good positions. When they finished one position, the association supported them until they could find another.

During the years that it existed, this association did a great deal of good. Well-to-do families sought these domestic workers and were always very satisfied with the services rendered. Mother Gamelin took special interest in them and they in turn showed to her the greatest confidence and affection.

St. James School was another project undertaken by Mother Gamelin at the request of Bishop Bourget. The school, located in the building that housed the printing presses of the "Mélanges Religieux", had been founded by Bishop Lartigue in 1827, for the poor children of the area and it offered free education. Lay teachers under the direction of the priests of the bishopric staffed it.

In October 1848, Mother Gamelin set out with Sister Caron for the beautiful little village of Saint Elizabeth in the county of Joliette to arrange with Father Quevillon, the Pastor, for the foundation of a convent there. The sisters at this new house would offer an elementary education to the girls as well as, care for the elderly and receive orphans. The sisters would also visit the poor and the sick in their homes.

On June 14, 1849 Mother Gamelin named the first sisters for this mission. As well she convened a general meeting of the women of the parish in order to form an Association of Ladies of Charity.

Mother Gamelin liked to attribute the success of her foundations to the protection of Our Lady of Seven Dolors. She had a particular and tender devotion to the passion of Our Lord and the Sorrows of His Blessed Mother and she never tired of instilling these devotions in her companions and her novices.

Therefore, the institution of any new practice in honor of these devotions filled her with profound joy. With great happiness then, in 1849 she welcomed the inauguration of the "Carnival Sanctified" in honor of Our Lady of Seven Dolors. Its aim was to make reparation for the sins committed during the worldly festivities of that time of the year. It was made during the thirty days prior to Ash Wednesday and it consisted of prayers to Our Mother of Sorrows, which were recited after the community Mass and followed by the simple Benediction of the Blessed Sacrament.

That same year, 1849, the plague, which had already, in 1832 and 1834, spread terror and death among the people, once again threatened Montreal. Cholera, after having made fearful ravages in Europe, invaded America. There was general panic. By early April, the epidemic had claimed several victims in Montreal. Those who fled to the countryside often carried the germs of contagion with them and fear became the instrument, which propagated the illness.

At the outset of the epidemic, Mother Gamelin went immediately to Bishop Bourget and asked that she be granted the favor of taking care of the sick; but he refused this request, because he did not wish to place in danger a life so valuable to the community.

The following night, a man knocked at the door of the asylum, loudly calling out for Sisters to come to the aid of his wife and two children who were dying of cholera. Mother Gamelin was filled with anguish. "How can I send someone?" she asked knowing that the person sent would likely be going to her death."

Deeply moved and her eyes full of tears, she went up to the dormitory and rang the bell to awaken the sisters, saying to them, " Sisters are needed to care for the cholera patients. Who will be the first to go?" "I, I" cried several rising without hesitation. A few minutes later, in the middle of that dark night, two sisters bravely set out to face the risk of death. They barely had time to assist the sick. In the morning they placed them in three coffins.

On the 30th of August 1849 the entire personnel of the asylum, assembled in the large hall of the elderly women to assist at a ceremony, which marked an important event in the history of the Community. Miss Rose Grandpré, in the presence of Bishop Prince, Vicar General Truteau, and Mother Gamelin, solemnly dedicated herself to the service of the poor as a lay auxiliary of the Institute. She was the first one to make this commitment and later on, she was clad in the distinctive dress of the Third Order of the Servites of Mary.

The Third Order of the Servites of Mary, originated with the religious order of the same name, in Italy around the end of the thirteenth century. Its foundation is attributed in a special way to Saint Juliana Falconieri, who was directed by Saint Philip Beniti, one of the founders of the Servite family.

Like the religious of the first order, the third order was instituted to honor in a special way the Sorrows of the Mother of God. The daughters of Saint Juliana devoted themselves to the care of the sick and to works of charity similar to those undertaken by the Sisters of Providence. For this reason Bishop Bourget was inspired with the idea of grafting onto the community of the Sisters of Providence founded by Mother Gamelin, a branch of the Third Order of the Servites of Mary.

The project was in perfect accord with the views of Mother Gamelin, who established at that time an association of lay sisters, thus creating valuable assistants to help the religious in their work.

The third order was officially inaugurated in the Institute on June 1, 1863, with the authorization of the General Superior of the Servites.[17]

On September 7, 1900, by a Decree of the Sacred Congregation of Religious, the Community of the Sisters of Providence was declared a Pontifical Institute, thus the affiliation to the third order of servites was suppressed and the tertiary sisters from then on were called "Coadjutrice Sisters".[18]

17. *Idem*, pages 201 to 214.
18. Archives of the Community.

SIMPLICITY, HOSPITALITY
Second Trip to the United States 1850

Mother Gamelin possessed to a high degree that Christian simplicity of soul that reveals itself without reticence or evasion and whose humility neither hid her weaknesses nor denied her faults. She practiced the same perfect honesty with herself as with others. This transparency was evident in her examination of conscience and in her openness with her spiritual directors. She would reveal to them her deepest feelings, laying open all the dispositions and sentiments of her heart in perfect confidence and sincerity, so that she might place herself under their guidance with all simplicity.

The religious of other communities, who visited the house, greatly appreciated the rare natural qualities of Mother Gamelin as well as her virtues, which they observed in the various actions of her daily life.

Mother Gamelin took great care to warmly welcome these religious. She liked to wait on them herself and sent her sisters to accompany them when they went into the city center. She placed all that she had at their disposal and their wants were anticipated with care and attention.

These visits gave her the opportunity of learning more about the various kinds of works and ministries accomplished by communities similar to her own, thus she was able to profit by the insights and experiences of others. She also shared her own personal views and experiences with them as well as those of her sisters, so that the visits and interviews were mutually advantageous.

The desire to gain exact information and practical knowledge about the organization of other charitable institutions had inspired Mother Gamelin and Bishop Bourget to travel to the United States, where Mother Gamelin visited the houses of the Daughters of Charity before her entrance into religious life in 1843.

The same desire inspired her to make a second trip of the same nature in the spring of 1850. The growth of her works and the foundation of new houses inspired her to once again have recourse to the experience of others in order to ensure the success of her undertakings. In this trip of five weeks duration, accompanied by Sister Ignace de Loyola, she visited the institutions of the Daughters of Charity in Albany, Baltimore, New York, and Emmitsburg. Everywhere she was received with the greatest kindness, finding in these houses, happy memories and the renewal of acquaintances made during her first visit.[19]

———

The boarding schools have been truly fruitful in their preparation of novices for religious life especially for our own Community. There, a great number of sisters are formed during their adolescence by piety and study. This early education developed in them those solid virtues, which are the best dowry for those who aspire to religious life.

———

19. *Idem*, pages 214 to 218.

THE FINAL YEAR
1851

February 19, 1851 the birthday of Mother Gamelin, saw the foundation at Long Pointe of a new project destined to be the last jewel in her earthly crown. It was the work of teaching deaf persons, a work, which came into being amid innumerable difficulties and contradictions.

There were many people who considered it a futile project as it seemed impossible to teach a person without hearing. Mother Gamelin persevered in her dream just the same.

March 29, 1851 was the seventh anniversary of the foundation of the Institute and Mother Gamelin wanted to celebrate with due solemnity. The memory of that never to be forgotten day inspired songs vibrant with joy and gratitude, but for Mother Gamelin they presaged the final vesper hymn.

Then at the end of May, Mother Gamelin undertook the official visitation of the houses she had founded. Besides the Mother House, there were seven others: Providence of Longue Pointe, Saint Joseph Hospice in Montreal, Providence at Laprairie, that of Saint Elizabeth, the Hospice of Saint Jerome Emilianus, Providence of Sorel, and Saint James School. Everywhere Mother Gamelin went she recommended to her sisters the love of the poor, union, mutual charity and confidence in God.

"Do not fear", she frequently repeated, "as long as you are surrounded by the poor, Providence will provide for everything and will be your faithful treasurer. Believe me, you will not want for anything."

At the beginning of September, while visiting the mission of Saint Elizabeth, which she specially loved on account of the gentle and amiable saint after whom it was named, she had a presentiment of her approaching death. The day after her arrival accompanied by Sister Caron and two Ladies of Charity, she went to call upon a benefactress of the convent, who lived at some distance from the village. The weather was fine but very warm.

Mother Gamelin insisted upon walking so that she might enjoy the beauties of nature, which she had always passionately loved and which helped her to lift her soul to God. After walking for about fifteen minutes, Mother Gamelin felt unusually fatigued so she sat down in the shade of a tree and said to her sisters in a tone of great sadness, "the atmosphere is heavy; it is cholera weather."

A few days later, tenderly taking leave of her sisters, she addressed them in these solemn words, "farewell, my dear daughters, I now see you for the last time. I have prayed to Saint Elizabeth that you may always love the poor, and that peace and union may ever be preserved among you". It was September 10. All eyes were filled with tears, but those present were far from thinking that the sad prophecy was so soon to be fulfilled.

On returning to the asylum, Mother Gamelin set to work to put all the business of the house in order. Up to this time, either the ecclesiastical superior or Bishop Bourget had presided over the council meetings of the community. Since Bishop Prince had recently resigned from the office of superior, Mother Gamelin insisted that Bishop Bourget be the one to preside over the next council meeting.

The Bishop answered by authorizing her to preside over all the council meetings in future, judging her perfectly capable of acquitting herself well in that function. This reply at first alarmed Mother Gamelin and the councilors, as it was customary at that time to receive direction in all their deliberations, from their ecclesiastical superiors. Never the less, they received this response filled with confidence, knowing that in fact it was another gesture of Providence that was guiding them in their journey.

In any case, the Bishop's decision was the beginning of a new epoch in the life of the Congregation. He seemed to affirm thereby that the sisters had acquired sufficient wisdom and experience to take greater initiative in managing their own affairs and in their internal governance.

Consequently, Mother Gamelin presided, for the first time and for the last, over the Council meeting of September 22, which was the last day of her life. Here again it seemed that God wanted to signify to the little family that its future was sufficiently assured so that God could take its first Superior and abandon them entirely to the guidance of Providence.

During that session, in which many questions were discussed, Mother Gamelin seemed to be deeply moved. She gave an urgent exhortation to the sisters on the duties and virtues of their state, recommending very specially charity towards the novices.

She left the session with her face lit up with an expression of joy and satisfaction. It seemed that she felt in the depths of her being a profound conviction that her work was solidly established, having successfully passed through the difficulties and painful uncertainties of its early beginnings. It seemed that her soul was inwardly singing its Nunc dimittis. It seemed as if God wished to illumine the last hours of her life that was mysteriously drawing to its close, with the first rays of that other life of peace and happiness so soon to dawn for her in eternity.

It was without doubt Our Lady of Seven Dolors, in whom Mother Gamelin had placed all her confidence, who filled her now with such peace and sweet serenity. It was this which shone resplendent on her countenance and gave Mother Gamelin unusual gaiety and vivacity.

The sisters remarked on it during the evening recreation. Never had Mother Gamelin appeared in better health or better spirits. There was no sign whatever of suffering or discomfort in her appearance or her manner. Nevertheless, it was Mother Gamelin's last evening; the night that followed was to reveal to her the approach and the bitterness of death.[20]

---

20. *Idem*, pages 220-231.

THE FINAL HOURS
September 23, 1851

About four in the morning, Mother Gamelin felt the first pangs of that deadly malady, the symptoms of which were so familiar to her. Immediately she called the sister who shared the room with her, and said, "My dear Sister, I am going to die; I have cholera. I wish to be taken up to the infirmary so as to die as the other sisters, who have gone before me, in the common room."

Some of the sisters, who were quickly awakened, carried her to the infirmary without being able, however, to share her apprehension. No one was willing to believe in the gravity of the illness nor in the imminence of the danger. But finally, they were obliged to accept the diagnosis and the opinion of two doctors who were called without delay.

Who could describe the fervent supplications addressed to God and to our Mother of Sorrows, for the preservation of such a precious life? The poor, the religious and the Ladies of Charity gathered one after another in the chapel, weeping, praying, and even offering their own life for Mother Gamelin, whose death would create so great a void. Nothing was spared in their efforts to move heaven and if their prayers were not heard, it was because God did not wish that this faithful servant should wait any longer for her eternal reward. Her crown was ready and the just and merciful Master was eager to address to Mother Gamelin those words of promise: "I was hungry and you gave me to eat; I was a prisoner and you visited me; I was naked and you clothed me. Come, then, to possess my kingdom for eternity."

Mother Gamelin had, during the whole course of her life, dreaded that terrible moment. Therefore, she felt at first a lively fear; but she very soon recovered profound peace, seeing in death only the will of God and the final threshold to be crossed in order to be fully united with God. The words of Saint Vincent de Paul were completed in her: "Whoever has loved the poor during life will have no fear at the hour of death."

Mother Gamelin asked to make her last confession to Bishop Prince, who had so often received her confidences and her avowals and restored peace to her soul. Then she had a long interview with Bishop Bourget who gave her the sacrament of the sick and the plenary indulgence. It is very rare in cases of cholera, but Mother Gamelin was able to receive the Holy Viaticum and she remained conscious until the last moment.

Around eleven o'clock in the morning, when the members of the Community were admitted to her presence, they could scarcely recognize her: her color was livid, her eyes sunken, her lips colorless. Mother Gamelin retained, nevertheless, full possession of her mind and seemed perfectly at peace.

She welcomed each of the sisters with motherly affection, and though unable to speak because of her extreme weakness, she embraced them all with her eyes, which expressed all her tenderness.

As her strength rapidly declined, Bishop Bourget began to recite the prayers for the dying to which Mother Gamelin responded by piously kissing the crucifix. When the prayers were ended, she murmured a few words in the Bishop's ear. It was her final recommendation to her sisters, which the devout prelate immediately transmitted, to them in a voice choked by emotion. "I convey to you", he said, "the testament of your Mother.

May it always be the basis of your perfection: humility, simplicity, and charity." "Above all," murmured Mother Gamelin as she was dying, "cha...ri..."

Mother Gamelin did not have strength to finish. Pressing the crucifix to her breast in a final movement, she breathed her last, murmuring the word "charity" which summed up her whole life as it sums up the gospel of Christ.

It was four o'clock in the afternoon.

It was Tuesday, September 23, 1851, the third day of the octave of the feast of Our Lady of Seven Dolors.

Mother Gamelin was fifty-one years, seven months and three days old. She had spent seven years in religious life.

Exactly twelve hours had sufficed to tear her away from this life and bring her to the eternal rest she had merited so well, and where she could sing in the presence of God: "O Providence Most Gentle!"[21]

---

21. *Idem*, pages 231 to 236.

Steps in the Cause for Beatification

1960	Historic Research
1977	Naming of the Postulator: Father Angelo Mitri, o.m.i.
1981	Official Decree for the Introduction of the Cause for Beatification in Montreal
1981	Study of the Documents by a Historical Commission
1983	Diocesan process on her life and her reputation for holiness
1989	Presentation of the book of the Positio in Rome
1993	Promulgation of the Decree of Venerability
1997	Diocesan enquiry on a miracle obtained through her intercession
1999	Positive vote by the Doctors in Rome on the Miracle
2000 (May)	Positive vote by the Theologians in Rome on the Miracle
2000 (Nov.)	Positive vote by the Cardinals in Rome on the Miracle
2000 (Dec.)	Decree on the Authenticity of the Miracle
2001 (Mar.)	Announcement of the Beatification
2001 (October 7)	Ceremony of the Beatification in Rome

Bibliography

Mère Gamelin, par une religieuse de la Providence, Eusèbe Sénécal et Cie, Montréal, 1900.

La femme au cœur attentif, Eugène Nadeau, o.m.i., Providence - Montréal, 1969.

Mère Gamelin, sa Cause de Béatification, Angelo Mitri, o.m.i., Providence - Montréal, 1978.

Un cœur qui bat, Irène Richer, s.p., Providence - Montréal, 1978.

Saint-Jacques de Montréal, Mgr Olivier Maurault, p.s.s., Au presbytère, Montréal, 1923.

Madame la duchesse de Bassano, Insigne bienfaitrice des Sœurs de la Providence, Montréal, 1923.

The Table of the King. The story of Mother Gamelin, Katherine Burton, Mc Mullen Books, New York, 1952.

TABLE OF CONTENTS